# Be Yourself
## Overcoming Social Anxiety

Carla Mooney

San Diego, CA

© 2025 ReferencePoint Press, Inc.
Printed in the United States

**For more information, contact:**
ReferencePoint Press, Inc.
PO Box 27779
San Diego, CA 92198
www.ReferencePointPress.com

ALL RIGHTS RESERVED.
No part of this work covered by the copyright hereon may be reproduced or used in any form or by any means—graphic, electronic, or mechanical, including photocopying, recording, taping, web distribution, or information storage retrieval systems—without the written permission of the publisher.

---

LIBRARY OF CONGRESS CATALOGING-IN-PUBLICATION DATA

---

Names: Mooney, Carla, 1970- author.
Title: Be yourself : overcoming social anxiety / Carla Mooney.
Description: San Diego, CA : ReferencePoint Press, Inc., 2024. | Includes
   bibliographical references and index.
Identifiers: LCCN 2024007351 (print) | LCCN 2024007352 (ebook) | ISBN
   9781678207885 (library binding) | ISBN 9781678207892 (ebook)
Subjects: LCSH: Social phobia--Juvenile literature.
Classification: LCC RC552.S62 M65 2024  (print) | LCC RC552.S62  (ebook) |
   DDC 616.85/225--dc23/eng/20240327
LC record available at https://lccn.loc.gov/2024007351
LC ebook record available at https://lccn.loc.gov/2024007352

# CONTENTS

## Introduction  4
A Struggle to Be Social

## Chapter One  8
Understanding Social Anxiety

## Chapter Two  20
Treatments and Strategies for Social Anxiety

## Chapter Three  32
Improving Social Skills

## Chapter Four  43
Living with Social Anxiety

| | |
|---|---|
| Source Notes | 54 |
| Getting Help and Information | 57 |
| Index | 60 |
| Picture Credits | 63 |
| About the Author | 64 |

# INTRODUCTION

# A Struggle to Be Social

For eighteen-year-old Jamie Factor, social anxiety has been a part of life for many years. Factor remembers being eleven years old and feeling the enormous pressure of anxiety every day before school. At the time, Factor did not have a name for her feelings. "I always connected it to the typical middle school angst, but I always knew it was more. I just wanted to avoid it. It wasn't the typical anxiety where tests made me nervous. I was more worried about who to sit next to on the bus or partner up with in class,"[1] she says.

When Factor started high school, she hoped her anxious feelings would disappear. She planned to enjoy her high school years and wanted to be part of school activities, make new friends, and have fun at parties. Yet Factor found it much more challenging than she thought it would be to meet new people. She tried attending a few club meetings but then stopped going. Instead of hanging out with friends on the weekends, Factor stayed home with her parents. She felt guilty about not participating in social activities. But at the same time, she was content staying home.

Over the next four years, Factor struggled to interact with others at school. "Every day before class, I would pray and hope that it would be an easy day—not where there wasn't work but a day when I could work alone,"[2] she recalls. One summer, she tried to attend a three-week summer program for high school students in California, but her social anxiety skyrocketed, and she left after four days.

After visiting her older brother at college, Factor hit a wall. She woke up one morning and told her parents she was not returning to school. "I was at my breaking point, and I wanted to die,"[3] she remembers. Factor's breakdown was a cry for help. She had tried therapy before for her anxiety but had not been serious about it. Now she started seeing a new therapist who taught her skills and recommended medication to manage her social anxiety and depression.

Slowly, Factor began gaining self-confidence and becoming more comfortable in social situations. She improved enough to attend a six-week writing program in New York City. "Sure, I was worried about a California repeat, but it was a trial for college, and I had to know if I could do it. I went from the shy 16-year-old unable to leave my house to a confident 18-year-old marching around the Big Apple," she says. Now, Factor is excited to go to college and for the future. And she is grateful that she found the help she needed to manage her social anxiety. "The amount of anxiety I would feel in normal social situations was crazy. I'm glad I got help because nobody should live the way I was living,"[4] she comments.

> "The amount of anxiety I would feel in normal social situations was crazy. I'm glad I got help because nobody should live the way I was living."[4]
>
> —Jamie Factor, a teen with social anxiety

## Living with Social Anxiety

Everyone gets nervous at times in social situations. Speaking in front of a large group or attending a party without a friend can trigger nerves. However, social anxiety is more than feeling nervous from time to time. For people with social anxiety, everyday social interactions can cause significant anxiety. They become overwhelmingly self-conscious and embarrassed in social situations because they fear people will look at or judge them negatively. "Very few people understand the agonizing and traumatic

> "Most people with social anxiety disorder try to hide it from others, especially from family and loved ones."[5]
>
> —Thomas A. Richards, a psychologist

depth of social anxiety disorder. Social anxiety makes people go inside themselves and try to 'protect' this secret. Most people with social anxiety disorder try to hide it from others, especially from family and loved ones,"[5] explains Thomas A. Richards, a psychologist and director at the Social Anxiety Institute.

Like Factor, many people struggle with social anxiety. In the United States, approximately 15 million adults are diagnosed with social anxiety disorder each year, according to the Anxiety & Depression Association of America. Many more, including teens and undiagnosed adults, are affected by social anxiety. The mental health condition affects men and women equally, and many people report first noticing symptoms as young teenagers.

*Everyday interactions can be very challenging for people who suffer from social anxiety. It can be alienating.*

## A Chronic and Treatable Condition

Without treatment, social anxiety can disrupt a person's life. Over time, avoiding social situations becomes easier than dealing with the negative feelings they provoke. "It makes me feel like I don't want to go out and talk to anyone. I would always rather stay at home and curl up on the sofa or bury myself in jobs around the house to distract myself from any social demands,"[6] says one person with social anxiety.

Avoiding social situations can negatively impact work, school, and relationships with family and friends. "It can affect you so broadly when you miss opportunities. When a person's isolated, it can lead to depression because you miss opportunities to have a good time or enjoy yourself and feel connected to other people,"[7] notes psychologist Dawn Potter.

The good news is that although social anxiety is a chronic mental health condition, it is treatable. Many people find that therapy, medication, and other coping skills can improve a person's ability to interact with others. With proper treatment, many people with social anxiety can live a full and productive life.

CHAPTER ONE

# Understanding Social Anxiety

In June 2021, twenty-five-year-old Nevandria Page moved to Ottawa, Canada, for graduate school. At first, Page was excited to explore Ottawa. She enjoyed eating out with friends and finding new restaurants and cafés. But Page soon started feeling anxious. "When we were out, I was feeling really nervous and anxious, and I felt like everyone was staring at me. It felt like I was really exposed and really vulnerable,"[8] she recalls.

Instead of enjoying her new school and city, Page dreaded leaving her house. Simply ordering coffee caused her to stutter. And while wearing blue box braids for the first time, she became highly self-conscious. Convinced that people were staring at her, Page hid next to a building and cried, anxious that others were judging her.

## More than Being Shy

Feeling overwhelmed in social situations or a large crowd is expected occasionally. Many people feel nervous before a date or a job interview. Some people are shy and take some time to warm up to new people. Social situations may make them self-conscious and uncomfortable. Yet these feelings usually fade as a person becomes more comfortable around new people and situations. When these feelings do not go away, a person may be experiencing social anxiety.

Most people experience social anxiety at some point in their lives. Social anxiety is driven by a fear of being judged by others. People who have social anxiety worry about what people—both friends and strangers—think about them. "There are times when experiencing social anxiety is normal, such as when we're about to meet someone new or give a speech,"[9] says Kevin Chapman, a licensed clinical psychologist. Worrying about what others think about a person is common in these situations. However, when these feelings last for months and interfere with daily life, a person may have a mental health condition called social anxiety disorder.

## A Mental Health Condition

Anxiety disorders induce in sufferers an extreme sense of dread or panic when facing uncomfortable situations. People with social anxiety disorder have a persistent fear of social situations in which they feel that others are judging them. "If someone is consistently experiencing a fear of social situations for six months or more, it's an indicator that they may have social anxiety disorder,"[10] comments Mailae Halstead, a licensed therapist at Connecticut's Behavior Wellness Clinic.

These fears can become so intense that they interfere with a person's ability to go to work or school or participate in everyday activities. Whereas some people will avoid these situations entirely, others will participate in them but suffer from significant fear and anxiety when they do. Social anxiety disorder can even cause worry weeks before an event is scheduled. For example, a person with social anxiety disorder may avoid going to the store or calling people on the phone.

> "If someone is consistently experiencing a fear of social situations for six months or more, it's an indicator that they may have social anxiety disorder."[10]
>
> —Mailae Halstead, a therapist

In its simplest terms, social anxiety is strongly linked to a fear of rejection, according to Fallon Goodman, an assistant professor of psychology at George Washington University. Everyone experiences rejection, from not getting into a dream college or landing a top job to getting turned down for a second date. For people with social anxiety disorder, rejection becomes part of how they see themselves. "You believe you were ghosted because you're not lovable enough. You believe you were turned down for that job because you're not intelligent enough," relates Goodman. And each rejection makes it harder for a person to put themselves out there and risk another rejection. "For some people, rejection is so painful, so traumatic, that they systematically avoid social interactions throughout their life,"[11] she says.

## Signs and Symptoms of Social Anxiety

Although each person's experience with social anxiety is unique, there are some common signs and symptoms. Most people with social anxiety display some avoidance behaviors. "This avoidance may be overt, such as skipping social events or calling in sick on the day they are to give a presentation, or it may be covert, such as attending a social event but spending most of the time scrolling through their phone, or giving the presentation but reading off a word-for-word script rather than connecting with the audience,"[12] states Ellen Hendriksen, a clinical psychologist at Boston University. Avoidance can also appear as wearing sunglasses to avoid eye contact, walking in a roundabout path to avoid running into people, or not being assertive.

Physically, people may sweat, blush, or tremble in uncomfortable social situations. Their heart may beat fast. Some people feel nauseated; others find that their mind has gone blank and cannot recall what they were going to say. In conversation or while giving a presentation, they may speak very softly or hold their body stiffly. Their mouth and throat may go dry and they may have trouble swallowing. Some people may experience panic attacks or even vomiting.

Emotionally, social situations trigger intense feelings of fear and self-consciousness in people with social anxiety. These feelings can make it difficult for them to interact with others. They worry about humiliating themselves before, during, and after events.

*Social anxiety can make even simple interactions, like calling someone on the phone, seem overwhelming.*

They are afraid that others will notice their anxiety. And they can be overly critical of themselves in social situations.

Sophie, a twenty-two-year-old college student, experienced social anxiety and its symptoms throughout school. "My heart hammered in my chest, and my palms were so sweaty that I felt like I had just run a mile. My first day at university was nerve-wracking, and I had even begun to question why I had thought it was a good idea to attend," she recalls, adding:

> Throughout my studies, I had always encountered the same response to crowded classrooms and the unbearable stares from my fellow students as I entered the room. I was yet to be diagnosed with social anxiety, but I had always preferred to keep my head down and to work unnoticed. There was always this fear at the very forefront of my mind that every time I entered a room, spoke,

or contributed, I was being negatively judged on how I looked, sounded, or—when my nerves really got the better of me—even on how I might have smelled.[13]

For some people, anxiety symptoms become so overwhelming that they avoid even everyday social situations. They decline invitations to parties and other social gatherings. They have trouble starting conversations or making eye contact. They may have trouble going to work or school. Eating in front of others, using a public restroom, talking to a store cashier, and even walking into a room where people are already sitting can be difficult, if not impossible, to do. Even just the anticipation of a future social situation can trigger intense fear and anxiety.

Social anxiety has caused Nanichi Hidalgo-Gonzales, a twenty-one-year-old student in Tallahassee, Florida, to dread leaving her home. In the past, Hidalgo-Gonzalez considered herself a social butterfly who enjoyed talking to people. Then the COVID-19 pandemic hit in 2020. Hidalgo-Gonzalez isolated at home and attended online classes like her peers. However, when school eventually returned to in-person classes, she was overwhelmed with social anxiety. She dreaded going to her in-person classes and rarely left home. Most of the time, she only ventured outside to get gas and groceries. "If I go out sometimes, I just feel like I'm in a bubble, and you're about to pop it," she says. On her birthday, Hidalgo-Gonzalez's friends planned a celebration at a restaurant. At the party, Hidalgo-Gonzalez struggled with feelings of nausea and claustrophobia and worried that she was going to have a panic attack. "I want to live my life; I want to experience this college thing. But then I feel like I just want to stay home because I don't want to go out and get anxious,"[14] she states.

Symptoms of social anxiety can change over time. They may become

> "I want to live my life; I want to experience this college thing. But then I feel like I just want to stay home because I don't want to go out and get anxious."[14]
> 
> —Nanichi Hidalgo-Gonzales, a college student with social anxiety

more intense during times of stress or life changes. Although avoiding situations that trigger social anxiety symptoms can feel better in the short term, the condition is likely to continue and may even worsen over time without treatment.

## Performance-Based Social Anxiety

Many people with social anxiety disorder feel uncomfortable with or completely avoid social situations, but some experience a form of social anxiety related to public speaking and performances. Situations such as giving a speech, being on stage, or competing in sports generate symptoms of anxiety. "It's performance-based only. You would have anxiety about public speaking, but wouldn't necessarily have anxiety about going to a party, ordering at a restaurant, or speaking on the phone to an unknown person,"[15] explains psychologist Dawn Potter.

*People with performance-based social anxiety are fine with everyday interactions, but may struggle with making presentations, sports, and other situations where they are the object of attention.*

Paddy, a seventeen-year-old rugby player, has experienced social anxiety linked to playing sports. When Paddy was eleven, he started playing rugby on his school team. Although he had been playing the sport for years, anxiety one day overwhelmed him. "Up until that point, I had been playing local club rugby, but playing for my school team, I had the feeling that I *had* to play well, and if I didn't, I would let my team down," he remarks. "I remember sitting in the [trunk] of my dad's car, and my dad asking me, 'Are you cold?' because my legs were shaking so much. The truth was my legs were shaking because of my anxiety about the game. But this did not start on the morning of the game. The nerves had been building up for days before." Paddy had trouble sleeping and eating days before a game. Even after a match, the feelings of anxiety remained, no matter if the team won or lost. Eventually, Paddy decided to take a break. "The negative emotions associated with playing became so overwhelming that I stopped playing rugby for six months,"[16] he says.

## Gut Microbes

Scientists from University College Cork in Ireland are studying whether gut microbes, the collection of bacteria and other organisms that live in a person's gastrointestinal system, play a role in social anxiety disorder. Recent research has found that when gut microbes from people with social anxiety disorder are placed into mice, the rodents display an increased response to social fear. These findings are consistent with other research showing a potential link between the gut biome and other conditions, such as depression. In the 2023 study, researchers tested social fear in mice by giving the mice small electric shocks when they got near a new mouse. Then, they observed how the mice behaved around new mice without shocks. Mice with gut microbes from healthy people regained their curiosity around new mice within a few days. However, mice with gut microbes from people with social anxiety disorder continued to show fear of new mice and never fully recovered their social skills. Additional analysis showed the two groups of mice had different levels of oxytocin, an important hormone in bonding. Scientists believe these results suggest that gut microbes play a role in social fear and social anxiety disorder.

## Causes of Social Anxiety

Like many mental health conditions, social anxiety disorder is not caused by one single factor. Instead, experts believe that a combination of genetic, biological, and environmental factors are involved in causing social anxiety disorder. "Some people can trace their social anxiety back to a terrible, horrible, no good, very embarrassing middle school or junior incident. Others may have a genetic predisposition for social anxiety. [It] can run in families,"[17] explains psychologist Angela Neal-Barnett.

People who have a family history of anxiety disorder are more likely to develop social anxiety disorder than those who do not. Scientists also suspect that changes in a person's brain structure and chemistry may increase the risk of developing anxiety disorders, including social anxiety. A 2019 study by researchers at the Cornell Weill School of Medicine and Yale University identified a specific neural circuit in the brain that appears to be linked to social anxiety disorder. The circuit connects the brain's cortex and the amygdala, its emotional center. When the circuit does not receive the proper amount of a protein called brain-derived neurotrophic factor (BDNF) during adolescence, vulnerability to social anxiety disorder increases. The researchers also noted that a shortage of BDNF is caused by a variation in the gene that controls its production.

Environmental factors may also increase the risk of social anxiety disorder. For example, having a negative or traumatic social experience can trigger a fear of social situations. As this fear progresses, it can become social anxiety disorder.

## Risk Factors

Although social anxiety disorder can affect anyone, some risk factors make a person more likely to develop the condition. People with parents or siblings who have or had social anxiety disorder are more likely to develop the disorder themselves. People who are shy, withdrawn, or restrained when put in new situations or when meeting new people have a greater risk of developing social anxiety disorder.

Adverse experiences may also be a risk factor for social anxiety disorder. Children who are teased, bullied, rejected, or humiliated may be at greater risk of developing the condition. Other adverse experiences, such as family conflict, trauma, or abuse, may also be risk factors for this disorder. People who are self-conscious about a physical condition such as a stutter or disfigurement may also be at greater risk of developing social anxiety disorder.

Social anxiety symptoms typically begin during late childhood or adolescence but can appear at any point in life. Sometimes, the pressure of giving a public speech, delivering a work presentation, or meeting new people can trigger social anxiety symptoms

*People who are self-conscious about a physical condition may be at greater risk of developing social anxiety disorder.*

in adults. Introverts may be more likely to develop social anxiety, but extroverts are not immune to this condition. Even people who are usually outgoing and talkative can become anxious when meeting new people or performing in front of large groups.

## Impact on Lives

People with social anxiety disorder experience an overwhelming fear that makes it difficult for them to participate in everyday activities. Most people affected by this condition understand that their fear is irrational. However, they are unable to move past their fear of social situations. Instead, they begin to avoid the situations that make them uncomfortable and create feelings of fear and anxiety. Untreated, the condition can get so bad that people struggling with social anxiety may withdraw from relationships, school, work, and other activities that they previously enjoyed. "Humans are hard-wired to connect with each other. But social anxiety gets in the way of people living the lives they want to live,"[18] comments Goodman.

> "Humans are hard-wired to connect with each other. But social anxiety gets in the way of people living the lives they want to live."[18]
>
> —Fallon Goodman, an assistant professor of psychology

Victoria Williams knows what it is like to have social anxiety affect relationships with friends. She explains,

> When I withdrew from social situations, stopped attending lessons, and spent most of my time having panic attacks or crying, I lost friends. Those I thought would always have my back, be there for me, and look after me . . . they turned away, saw me as "the girl who always cries"— a hassle. I can't lie: I let it affect me. My mind was already telling me I was a burden to everyone, and this was the proof my mental illness needed.

However, Williams is thankful for the friends who stuck by her side as she battled her anxiety. Simple texts or phone calls from them to check in on her and show they cared helped her tremendously. "Some of the strongest friendships I now have came out of this dreadful situation. I realized who my true friends were,"[19] she says.

For Amy, social anxiety in her teens and twenties made dating feel almost impossible for many years. Once, she reluctantly agreed to a date with a young man she had met at a youth leadership camp. As she drove to meet him, Amy's social anxiety flared:

> I remember that drive was the longest drive of my life. And I just felt physically sick. . . . I had to pull the car over. And I was hysterical, just sobbing. And I called my mom, and I said, I would rather die than go on this date, right now. It sounds so dramatic, in hindsight, but at that moment in time, I honestly would have preferred [to die], that's the state I was in. I just could not see a way through it.[20]

## Introversion Versus Social Anxiety

Extroverted people are naturally outgoing and enjoy socializing and sharing their thoughts and feelings with others. In comparison, introverts need time alone to recharge and feel confident about themselves; they enjoy quiet and calm. At first glance, introverts and people with social anxiety can appear similar. Both seek solitude and are often quiet in large groups when they go out at all. But introversion and social anxiety are not related. Introversion is a personality trait. Introverts are exhausted by large gatherings of people. They stay home because they want to, not because they are afraid of going out. In comparison, social anxiety is not a personality trait; it is a mental health condition. In social anxiety, fear drives a person to avoid social situations. Rakshitha Arni Ravishankar knows firsthand the difference between introversion and social anxiety. "I'm an introvert, and I love the quiet. But the time I spend with myself is hardly ever peaceful. When I'm alone, my mind inevitably conjures worst-case scenarios about the future and fixates on painful past memories. It loves to remind me of all the awkward, embarrassing, or uncomfortable moments I've stumbled through in life," she says.

Rakshitha Arni Ravishankar, "How I Manage My Social Anxiety at Work," *Harvard Business Review*, April 12, 2022. https://hbr.org.

Eventually, Amy worked through her social anxiety with a therapist and was able to overcome her fear of dating. Today, she has been together with her partner, Chris, for five years.

Untreated social anxiety can harm a person's health. As people avoid social interactions, they become increasingly isolated and can dwell on negative feelings, which increases the risk of developing depression and other mental health conditions. People with social anxiety disorder are also at higher risk of alcohol or drug abuse if they use these substances to escape their negative thoughts and feelings.

Social anxiety disorder is much more than simply being shy. It is a mental health condition that can cause a person to retreat from the interactions of everyday life. For people with social anxiety disorder, the fear of being embarrassed or judged can impact relationships, affect performance at school and work, and prevent them from doing activities they enjoy.

## CHAPTER TWO

# Treatments and Strategies for Social Anxiety

Social anxiety can feel overwhelming. However, like other mental health conditions, social anxiety disorder is treatable. Treatment can look different for everyone, but for many, it includes therapy. Other standard treatment options include medication, support groups, mindfulness techniques, and lifestyle changes.

## Therapy Works

For many individuals, therapy is a key component of any treatment plan to overcome social anxiety. A type of psychotherapy called cognitive behavioral therapy (CBT) is commonly used to treat social anxiety disorder. A mental health professional helps people with social anxiety examine their thoughts and emotions in CBT. With the professional's guidance, they learn to identify and challenge negative thoughts and how thoughts affect their behavior. They learn how to change their thoughts and feelings about stressful situations and embrace healthier thoughts and behaviors. Dawn Potter notes,

> With social anxiety specifically, you want to identify patterns of thinking that cause you to avoid social situations—like if a person's always expecting

the worst outcome or a person is fixated on the fact that someone might see them blushing, or sweating, or stammering. You want to help them learn to challenge those expectations and adopt more positive self-talk rather than negative self-talk.[21]

According to mental health experts, CBT is a very effective treatment to help a person overcome social anxiety disorder and several other mental health conditions. "With CBT, you teach the client what social anxiety is and where their fears are coming from," comments Kevin Chapman. For example, a person may be afraid of being embarrassed in social situations. In CBT, "the therapist helps the person replace those thoughts with evidence-based thoughts," says Chapman. The therapist asks the person, "What is the evidence that you will make a fool of yourself?"[22] The therapist usually helps people see that there is no evidence to support the fear. If people with social anxiety have experienced an embarrassing social situation, CBT helps them realize they overcame it. As a result, they learn to change the patterns of thoughts, emotions, and behaviors disrupting their lives.

Kristen Rogers, an adult with society anxiety, knows the impact CBT can have on the life of someone with the disorder. For many years, Rogers struggled with social anxiety on her own. It negatively impacted many parts of her life, from her friendships to her work performance. Finally, in 2020, she decided to seek professional treatment. "I realized trying to fix my social anxiety on my own wasn't working. I wanted to feel normal and not ruin my chances at a career, relationships, or friendships," she explains. She began CBT sessions with a therapist. "I had CBT assignments to complete and discuss with my therapist, who helped me integrate these lessons into my daily life. It wasn't easy," she admits. Through CBT, Rogers learned to challenge her negative thoughts and replace them with positive ones. Progress

> "I realized trying to fix my social anxiety on my own wasn't working. I wanted to feel normal and not ruin my chances at a career, relationships, or friendships."[23]
>
> —Kristen Rogers, an adult with social anxiety

was slow at times. "Positive changes didn't happen overnight—I occasionally noticed small improvements, but realizing total change has been more like painting a wall with thin layer over thin layer until the wall's saturated in color—you don't notice the difference until it's a total 180 degrees from what it used to be," she says. Today, Rogers enjoys spending time with friends and coworkers. "I still fumble in social settings now and then. Don't we all? But the difference between my pre- and during-CBT self is that now, I laugh off my moments of social awkwardness instead of ruminating over them for days,"[23] she says.

## Exposure Therapy

One part of CBT is participating in social situations and learning how to overcome the fear and anxiety these situations cause. This technique, called exposure therapy, gradually exposes people to situations they have avoided. It allows them to confront their fears slowly and in a controlled way. "Exposure therapy helps you learn to manage your emotions in a variety of triggering situations and reduce social anxiety symptoms. In short, exposure therapy can help rewire your brain's response to fear-inducing stimuli,"[24] explains Karmen Smith, a clinical social worker.

First, these individuals will identify situations that cause social anxiety. They will talk with their therapists about what it will be like to be in that situation. Their therapists may have them visualize being in that social situation and recognize any feelings that surface. Together with the therapist, they will discuss how to handle those feelings and their behavior in the situation.

Next, the individuals will expose themselves to social situations they find to be mildly uncomfortable. They may go to a store, watch a movie in a theater, or call a stranger. Sometimes, the therapist will go with them to provide support. "You don't have to go crazy and face your biggest fears all at once. It is actually best

Therapy is a key component of any plan to overcome social anxiety, particularly if the disorder significantly impacts a person's functioning in public places or other areas of life.

to start with situations that are only mildly uncomfortable and then to gradually work up to those that might have previously sent you into all-out panic,"25 says psychologist Victoria Shaw.

Gradually, individuals in exposure therapy participate in increasingly uncomfortable social situations. Often, they will repeat exposures in different settings until they become more comfortable handling it without becoming overanxious. They progressively navigate situations that used to make them highly uncomfortable. As they experience repeated success handling each social exposure and confronting their fears, their feelings of fear and discomfort decline. "The more we expose ourselves to the situations that we fear, the more comfortable we become navigating them,"26 notes Shaw.

> "The more we expose ourselves to the situations that we fear, the more comfortable we become navigating them."26
>
> —Victoria Shaw, a psychologist

## Medication

In some cases, mental health professionals prescribe medication to treat people with anxiety disorders, including social anxiety disorder. Some of the most common medications prescribed for social anxiety disorder are selective serotonin reuptake inhibitors (SSRIs). SSRIs are also commonly prescribed to treat depression. SSRIs are safe, effective, and often well tolerated by individuals. SSRIs block the reabsorption of the neurotransmitter serotonin in the brain, increasing serotonin levels. Serotonin is a neurotransmitter that carries messages between nerve cells in the brain and body. Serotonin plays an important role in a person's mood, and a lack of serotonin has been linked to depression, anxiety, and other mental health conditions.

*It is important to seek medical attention to get a proper diagnosis and form a treatment plan with your doctor. Sometimes a combination of therapy and medication can be effective.*

Another type of medication, serotonin-norepinephrine reuptake inhibitors (SNRIs), can also be used to treat social anxiety disorder. SNRIs block the reabsorption of the neurotransmitters serotonin and norepinephrine in the brain. Increasing the levels of these neurotransmitters can help regulate mood and relieve anxiety.

When taking SSRIs and SNRIs, doctors say that patience is key because these medications can take several weeks to start working. People taking these medications may also experience side effects such as headaches, nausea, or trouble sleeping. Typically, doctors will start individuals on a low dose of the medication to see how they tolerate it. The doctor may increase the dose slowly until the optimal dosage is achieved.

Beta-blockers are another type of medication used to treat social anxiety disorder. Beta-blockers address the physical symptoms people may experience, such as tremors, rapid heart rate, and sweating. Beta-blockers are commonly prescribed for people with performance-based social anxiety.

Benzodiazepines, a type of anxiety medication, are potent depressant drugs sometimes used to treat anxiety disorders, including social anxiety. These medications work quickly to reduce the symptoms of anxiety. However, with repeated use, people can develop a tolerance to the drug and need increasingly higher doses to get the same effects. As a result, doctors usually only prescribe benzodiazepines for a short time.

Each person reacts differently to medication. A medication that works for one individual may not be effective for another. Working with a mental health professional, many people try different medications, doses, or combinations of medications before they determine what is most effective for them. When used in combination with therapy, medication can be an effective part of a treatment plan for people with social anxiety disorder.

## Group Therapy and Support Groups

For people with social anxiety, the idea of meeting with others for group therapy or support may be highly uncomfortable. However, some people have found this type of treatment to be very effective in helping them manage their anxiety. Group therapy provides a place to face social fears in a safe, nonjudgmental place surrounded by people who understand what it feels like to have social anxiety.

Led by a mental health professional, group therapy brings people together to help them learn social skills in a safe environment. Group members can use role-playing to practice social situations, learn to make eye contact with others, and practice social skills. Group therapy often uses CBT to help participants learn how their thoughts, feelings, and behaviors are connected. It also uses elements of exposure therapy to slowly help participants practice social situations in a safe, controlled setting.

Marsha found group therapy helped her manage her social anxiety. For most of her life, she battled social anxiety. She skipped parties in high school and college, avoided public speaking, and declined social gatherings. "I spent most of my time in my dorm room or the library. I missed out on a lot," she recalls. When her therapist suggested she try a weekly therapy group, Marsha was initially resistant. Eventually, she agreed to join a group. Quickly, Marsha realized she had found a safe place with people who cared about each other and what they were experiencing. "People were thoughtful and mindful. They really listened. It wasn't like any group of people that I had experienced," she explains. Week by week, Marsha slowly opened up to the group and discussed her fears and stresses. Over time, Marsha felt better able to manage her social anxiety. Her friends noticed the positive changes in her. "I was more expressive, more outspoken. I wasn't afraid to disagree or address conflict. Group gave me the skills I needed. At work events, I even became an expert mingler,"[27] she says.

Some people find support groups helpful. Unlike group therapy, support groups are usually not led by a trained mental health professional and do not provide CBT or other types of therapy exercises. Instead, participants learn from each other as they share experiences, challenges, stresses, and successes. "It's an extremely safe place to open up about your experience because you know the others there are experiencing it too,"[28] says Chapman.

## Mindfulness and Meditation

When social anxiety feels overwhelming, mindfulness practices and meditation may help people relieve symptoms and reduce anxiety. Mindfulness is the practice of paying attention and being present. Mindfulness can help people pay attention to their thoughts and feelings to better understand how they react to situations that trigger anxiety.

Meditation is one form of mindfulness practice. During mindful meditation, individuals focus on what they are thinking and feeling at that moment. A mindful meditation session may start by sitting in a comfortable position. Practitioners breathe slowly and regularly through the nose, focusing on each breath moving in and out of the body. As thoughts and sensations interrupt, they note them

## Acceptance and Commitment Therapy

Acceptance and commitment therapy (ACT) is a form of psychotherapy that can be used to treat social anxiety disorder. In ACT, people with anxiety learn to stop avoiding, denying, and struggling with emotions. Instead, they are taught to accept that these feelings are an appropriate response to certain situations. They also learn these feelings should not prevent them from living their lives. "One of the primary benefits of ACT is that it helps individuals build a different relationship with their internal experiences. This means learning to relate to oneself and one's inner narrator with kindness and gentleness," says Avigail Lev, a clinical psychologist. With this perspective, people in ACT use mindfulness and goal-setting techniques to reduce their anxiety and discomfort in social situations. They pledge to make positive changes to their behaviors regardless of their feelings.

ACT was developed during the 1980s by Steven Hayes, a psychologist who had personal experiences with panic attacks. Determined to stop running from his panic attacks, Hayes developed ACT as a method to help others like him accept themselves and their experiences.

Deborah R. Glasofer, "What Is Acceptance and Commitment Therapy (ACT)?," Verywell Mind, January 16, 2024. www.verywellmind.com.

and refocus on their breathing. They may also incorporate guided imagery and other practices to relax the mind and body.

Over time, mindfulness meditation can also teach people to observe their thoughts and emotions without judging themselves. They become more self-aware and better understand what triggers anxiety and how to respond to it. Mindfulness meditation can also help people manage their feelings more easily and encourage them to be more self-compassionate. This can reduce anxiety-fueled negative thoughts.

Mindfulness meditation has proved effective for several mental health conditions, including depressive and anxiety disorders. Mindfulness meditation lowers stress, improves relaxation, and creates a calmer state, which makes it easier to manage triggering social situations. Physically, it can reduce a person's heart rate and blood pressure, both of which are physical symptoms of anxiety. For many people, mindfulness meditation is most successful in treating social anxiety when it is part of a larger approach that may include therapy, medication, and lifestyle changes.

## Lifestyle Changes

A healthy lifestyle can also help people manage social anxiety and other mental health conditions. For example, regular exercise can help reduce social anxiety. "Exercise has a profound effect on managing anxiety in general because the body is experiencing the same arousal response during exercise as with anxiety," states Chapman. In social situations, "this makes experiencing that arousal response less threatening."[29] For Ian Chew, regular exercise is an essential part of managing his social anxiety. "The mind is connected to the body in so many ways," he says. "Having worked out 4–5 times a week for the last three years, I've seen how exercise makes me more confident on good days and less anxious on bad days."[30]

Getting enough sleep, eating a healthy diet, and avoiding drugs and alcohol can also help reduce anxiety and take care of mental health. For example, if people do not get adequate sleep,

*A healthy lifestyle that includes regular exercise can help people manage social anxiety and other mental health conditions.*

their cortisol levels can rise. Cortisol is a hormone linked to stress and has a powerful influence on the body's sleep cycles. People's cortisol levels rise when stressed, and they can become more anxious. If cortisol levels are too high, especially in the evening, people may have trouble falling or staying asleep, and the cycle continues.

## Overcoming Social Anxiety

Ever since she was a child, Amy has struggled with social anxiety. As she got older, her anxiety increasingly interfered with her ability to participate in everyday activities. She avoided social situations and parties because they filled her with dread. In high school, Amy agreed to go to a school debutante ball with a friend. She was uncomfortable with the dance, but the thought of attending the after-party was overwhelming. She was obsessed with what people would think about her and what they would say behind her back if she did not attend. "My thoughts would lead from something bad to something terrible to something catastrophic. And it would go on and on and on. And before I knew it, I'd be thinking there's no way you're getting out of that party alive,"[31] she says. Amy skipped the party.

Over the next several years, Amy tried to manage her social anxiety on her own. Most of the time, she avoided social situations that made her feel uncomfortable. As she increasingly isolated herself, Amy felt like she was missing out on life. Yet she felt helpless to do anything about it.

That changed after Amy experienced a hysterical panic attack about going to work. The episode caused her to realize that she needed help, and she started seeing a psychologist. Together, they created a mental health plan that included CBT. Engaging in CBT, Amy worked through her anxiety over social situations. She slowly began attending more social activities, starting with daytime activities with a few friends. Amy worked up to attending parties and going to nightclubs, which had triggered massive anxiety in the past. She used strategies that she had learned and practiced in therapy, breathing techniques, and the support of friends to help her. Slowly, Amy's confidence rose, and her social

## Getting Help: Diagnoses and Treatment Plans

When social anxiety begins to disrupt a person's life and causes problems at school or work or in relationships with family and friends, many people reach out for professional help. A health care professional can diagnose a person with social anxiety disorder. First, health professionals will rule out other conditions that might be causing anxiety symptoms. To do this, they will perform a physical exam to determine whether there is any underlying medical condition or medication causing symptoms. They may order blood tests to check hormone and vitamin levels and other metabolic indicators that could signal there is an underlying condition causing anxiety symptoms. They will talk with individuals about symptoms, including frequency, and situations that trigger them. They may also have the client complete a questionnaire about their symptoms. After reviewing all the information, they will make a diagnosis and come up with a treatment plan.

anxiety declined. "Engaging in and committing to my therapy was key," Amy states. "It wasn't easy—at times, it was really confronting. The strategies took practice, and I definitely didn't get better overnight, but it was worth the effort. Back then, I never imagined my life could look like it does now, and I'm so proud of the hard work I did to get here."[32]

Although social anxiety can be a serious mental health condition, treatment is possible. Therapy, medication, lifestyle changes, and mindfulness practices can help people learn to manage and overcome anxiety in social situations. Claire Eastham was twenty-four years old when she was diagnosed with social anxiety disorder. She felt relieved to finally have a name for what she had been struggling with for years and find a treatment plan:

> "Never suffer with mental illness in silence. The situation might feel hopeless, but there is always something that can be done."[33]
>
> —Claire, a young adult with social anxiety

> I was prescribed medication, a course of CBT therapy, and was signed off work for one month. This allowed me to heal. For the first time in my life, I didn't feel so helpless. Social anxiety is something that can be controlled. Six years on, and I'm doing just that. I'd be lying if I said that I was cured, but I am happy and no longer a slave to my condition. Never suffer with mental illness in silence. The situation might feel hopeless, but there is always something that can be done.[33]

## CHAPTER THREE

# Improving Social Skills

For someone with social anxiety, interacting with people can be difficult. Social anxiety can stop people from participating in social situations because they fear being rejected or embarrassed. Even with treatment, these individuals may struggle with the social skills used to connect with others. As they learn to manage their anxiety, they may still find it challenging to start a conversation, identify social cues, be assertive, or read body language. With practice, however, people with social anxiety can overcome these challenges and improve their social skills.

## What Are Social Skills?

Social skills are the verbal and nonverbal communication skills people use to build connections with others and manage social situations. People are not born with social skills; instead, they learn these skills as they interact with others. Some individuals are very comfortable with social skills and quickly master them. For others, social skills do not come as naturally and are more challenging to learn. People who are shy or introverted may be uncomfortable using social skills and being in social situations. Others with social anxiety may also have trouble feeling comfortable with social skills.

    The more people practice social skills, the better they use them. Improving social skills has a lot of benefits. People use these skills to form strong bonds with others. Individuals with strong social ties have improved mental health and lower rates of depression and anxiety. They also have higher self-esteem and more empathy. Social ties can protect people's health as they age. Scientists have found that social isolation increases the risk of dementia in older adults.

When individuals avoid social situations because of anxiety, they miss out on opportunities to develop strong communication skills and build confidence. For example, people with social anxiety may avoid parties because they feel uncomfortable. The more they avoid parties, the fewer opportunities they have to develop strong communication skills and build confidence in social situations. Because avoidance never lets them practice navigating a social event, these individuals fail to learn how to manage such situations. Even if the individuals have the social skills to interact appropriately, they may not be confident about using them. Therefore, improving social skills and building confidence are critical to successfully managing social anxiety.

## Communication Skills

Verbal and nonverbal communication skills are essential to forming strong social connections. No one is born knowing how to communicate. Instead, people learn through practice and trial and error. "Communication is about more than just speaking. Like any new experience, there may be stress and the occasional gaffe when you first start, and it's important to recognize that this is normal. By merely being present, things will improve, sometimes invisibly, as you become more accustomed to social situations,"[34] explains Arlin Cuncic, a mental health expert specializing in social anxiety.

For a person with social anxiety, starting a conversation and keeping it going may feel like an impossible task. Engaging in small talk is challenging for some because they struggle to come up with things to say. Other people go to the other extreme and talk too much when anxious, which can inhibit a conversation. "The art of conversation may seem like a puzzle if

> "The art of conversation may seem like a puzzle if you have social anxiety disorder."[35]
>
> —Arlin Cuncic, a mental health expert

you have social anxiety disorder. You probably have trouble knowing what to say or feel uncomfortable talking about yourself. But, conversations are foundational to building relationships, and knowing how to better navigate them will help you get acquainted with those around you,"[35] says Cuncic.

Having a conversation is a skill like any other skill; it gets better with practice. People with social anxiety might find it easier to locate friends or colleagues in social settings so there is less fear in conversing. Finding one or two familiar faces in a crowded room can also be just the start a person needs to join a conversation. If a person does not know anyone in the room, one of the easiest ways to start a conversation is to introduce oneself. Remaining polite and not interrupting other people when they are talking are important tactics when joining and continuing a conversation.

*Social skills do not come naturally to some people. A lack of social skills can lead to anxiety about participating in social situations.*

Like many people with social anxiety, Claire Eastham dreads going to a party where she knows few people. "At first, I thought approaching people would be impossible for me: A sea of faces that I didn't recognize, all deep in conversation. I could never hope to be accepted," she says. However, Eastham knows that it is not something she can avoid, whether it is a work event or a dinner with a friend's family. To be successful, Eastham uses a few strategies to help her enter conversations. She suggests the following tactic:

> Approach two or three people and be honest: "I'm so sorry to interrupt, it's just that I don't know anyone here, and I was wondering if I could join your conversation?" It's daunting, but try and remember that people are . . . well, human! Empathy is a strong emotion, and unless they're completely bonkers—in which case, you're better off not talking to them—then they'll be glad to accept you.

The technique has been very successful for Eastham. She recalls, "The last time I tried this, a girl openly admitted: 'I'm so glad you said that, I don't really know anyone, either!'"[36]

Some people find that preparing conversation starters in advance can help when they are nervous. A lot of people start a conversation by commenting on the weather. Arts and entertainment topics are also good conversation starters. Books, movies, restaurants, and television shows can be simple ways to find common ground with others and start a conversation. Other good conversation-starter topics include sports, hobbies, travel, work, and hometowns. Many people enjoy discussing these topics, making it easier to build a conversation. "Remember that small talk is about building a bridge between you and another person. It doesn't matter so much what you talk about, but rather that you start talking,"[37] stresses Cuncic.

## Active Listening Skills

A conversation is not just one person talking all the time. Good conversations have a give-and-take, with people taking turns talking and listening. Therefore, active listening skills are an essential part of communication skills. Active listening means paying attention when another person speaks, asking questions about what they say, and thinking about what the other person said. People who actively listen in a conversation are not ignoring others or zoning out; they show the other people in the conversation that they are being heard.

When people actively listen, they are fully present in a conversation. Individuals who check their cell phones in the middle of a conversation signal that they are not fully present. Instead, putting away phones and other distractions allows people to give their full attention to a conversation. Also, people's nonverbal cues can sig-

*Talking with someone new can feel intimidating to someone with social anxiety disorder. But like any skill, this one improves with practice.*

nal that they are fully present in a conversation. Smiling while listening, leaning toward a speaker, and nodding at appropriate points are all nonverbal behaviors that show a person is actively listening.

Making eye contact is an essential part of active listening. Making eye contact with others in a conversation shows that the individual is focused and listening to what is being said. If, instead, these individuals are constantly looking around, it appears as if they are distracted by people or activity outside of the conversation. However, too much eye contact can make people feel uncomfortable. Therefore, communications experts recommend that people who are good at active listening aim to make eye contact for intervals of three to four seconds during a conversation.

Asking questions is another way people show they are actively listening and paying attention in a conversation. The best questions are open-ended ones that need more than a "yes" or "no" answer. Open-ended questions keep a conversation moving. "Open-ended questions encourage thoughtful, expansive responses, which is why they are often used by mental health therapists,"[38] notes Cuncic.

Active listening also involves being patient and reflecting on what others are saying. Good active listeners do not interrupt; they let speakers finish their thoughts. They also reflect on what they hear. One way to do this is by paraphrasing or summarizing what others have just said. For example, Boston University's ombuds office suggests using statements like "It sounds like what is most important to you is . . . ," "What I'm hearing is . . .," or "If I'm hearing you correctly . . ."[39] to indicate active listening.

Active listeners pay attention to fully understand what others are saying and are not in a hurry to respond. "How many times have you caught yourself listening to someone, with an agenda already mapped out in your head? Before they even manage to complete the sentence, you are ready to interject with your response or to take the conversation elsewhere. This tells the other person that all you care about is what you have to say," comments Rachel Wells, an entrepreneur and leadership expert.

Wells recommends avoiding quick responses during a conversation and instead taking the time to respond thoughtfully. "The next time you are in conversation or a 1:1 meeting, pause, hold back that thought, and genuinely hear the other person out. Seek to understand their point of view and [to discover] the message behind what they're verbally expressing. Then tailor your responses with that in mind,"[40] she says.

## Nonverbal Communication Skills

People can say a lot without words. Their body movements, facial expressions, mouth movements, eye contact, gestures, posture, and tone of voice all communicate information. For example, tone of voice can reveal if a speaker is happy or stressed. People who bite their lip may be anxious, worried, or stressed. Others who stand with hands on hips may signal confidence.

People with social anxiety often display body language that makes them appear unfriendly. They might cross their arms, which can make them appear closed off and unapproachable. Crossed legs can also signal a person is uncomfortable or closed

### The Importance of Empathy

Empathy, the ability to notice, understand, and share another person's emotions, is an important social skill. In many ways, empathy is the foundation for all other social skills. Empathy helps people communicate. It enables people to connect with each other, be compassionate, and develop strong relationships. People who lack empathy may have difficulty in social situations, struggle to make friends, and have a hard time working with others. They might say or do something that appears rude or inappropriate to others. They might say things that hurt others' feelings or do things that are viewed negatively, such as cutting to the front of a line. Sometimes, people with anxiety disorder may appear to lack empathy because they appear withdrawn and hesitant to engage with others. However, the two should not be confused. People with anxiety might simply not be adept at expressing their emotions. But like other social skills, empathy can be practiced and more deeply developed.

off. They may display a closed posture by hunching forward and crossing their arms and legs. This posture hides the body and can send signals of anxiety and unfriendliness.

Sometimes, people with social anxiety rely on certain behaviors in public situations to prevent others from noticing their anxiety. They may wear sunglasses or earbuds to avoid interacting with others. They may spend much time scrolling through a cell phone to avoid talking to others. These nonverbal actions may help them reduce their anxiety, but they send a message to others of being aloof or unapproachable.

> "By paying closer attention to other people's unspoken behaviors, you will improve your own ability to communicate nonverbally."[41]
>
> —Kendra Cherry, a psychosocial rehabilitation specialist

In contrast, positive body language can signal interest and engagement. People who stand with an upright, open posture signal friendliness, openness, and willingness. They maintain good eye contact during a conversation. They smile and nod while actively listening.

Noticing how others use nonverbal cues in communication can help people improve their own nonverbal communication. "By paying closer attention to other people's unspoken behaviors, you will improve your own ability to communicate nonverbally,"[41] says Kendra Cherry, a psychosocial rehabilitation specialist. Instead of looking at the floor during a conversation, a person might show interest and engagement by making eye contact with the speaker while adopting an appropriate facial expression.

## Assertiveness

Many people with social anxiety find speaking up for themselves to be very difficult. For example, a new college student may avoid talking to a roommate about being noisy late at night. Instead of talking to the roommate about being quieter after a specific time, the college student puts up with being woken up regularly. To avoid conflict, such people put their own needs

## Just Smile

Smiling is something many people do every day without thinking. For people with social anxiety who are dealing with anxious thoughts and fears, smiling can be difficult. Yet smiling may be just what they need. Studies have shown that smiling increases mood-lifting hormones in the body while decreasing stress hormones such as cortisol. Smiling also reduces blood pressure. And smiling also uses muscles that trigger the brain to produce endorphins and other chemicals that boost mood, relax the body, and reduce pain. Smiling also makes a person appear more confident and approachable. "I began smiling at strangers when I went out in public and noticed how relaxed I was when I got home," comments Alexa Shea, who battles social anxiety. "In my mind, I was smiling as a way to tell people I was non-threatening, kind, maybe even a cool person to know. Lo and behold, seeing their smile in return eased my own mind; quelling my anxiety." Even if a smile is forced, it can have a positive impact on the mind and body.

Alexa Shea, "Smiling at Strangers Was a Helpful Tool for My Social Anxiety," Byrdie, November 3, 2021. www.byrdie.com.

---

aside and defer to what others want. Yet doing so can increase feelings of anxiety, depression, and helplessness. They become frustrated and sometimes dislike themselves for being unable to speak up.

Assertive communication does not mean picking a fight with every person in the room. Instead, assertive communication is being straightforward and open about what one thinks, feels, needs, and wants. It allows people to be open about their own needs while still being respectful and considerate of the needs of others. Assertive communication is an essential social skill.

People who speak up for themselves effectively often use statements that begin with the word "I" and pair it with a verb that directly describes their thoughts or feelings. For example, they may say, "I like Italian food" or "I feel hurt that you left the party without me." For people with social anxiety, being more assertive will feel uncomfortable at first. However, with practice it will help reduce anxiety and improve communication.

Julie, an adult with social anxiety, role-played assertiveness skills with her therapy group. Practicing in a safe space with group members helped her be more assertive. "Doing assertion role plays helped me feel more confident in the real world. Staying calm while standing up to someone who is (acting) rude and mean . . . helped me to be a little more assertive in real life,"[42] she explains.

> "Doing assertion role plays helped me feel more confident in the real world."[42]
>
> —Julie, an adult with social anxiety

## Social Skills Training

Although most people learn social skills from their family and friends, others prefer to hone these skills with a mental health professional. Social skills training (SST) is a type of therapy that has been successfully used to improve the social skills of people with mental health conditions, including social anxiety

*One-on-one or group social skills training can make people more confident in social situations and reduce anxiety.*

disorder. A person may work one-on-one with a therapist or in a group setting.

SST uses various methods, including role-play, rehearsal, feedback, and positive reinforcement, to help people develop the social skills they use in everyday situations. Sometimes, a person does not lack social skills but needs to learn how to use them effectively. Rahan Ali, a clinical psychologist, occasionally uses SST as one part of a treatment program for people with social anxiety disorder. In his experience, SST makes sense because it can be customized for each person's needs. "We don't work with this idea that we all have the same interpersonal style. It's not about altering who you are . . . but recognizing a specific problem and using this tool to address it,"[43] he states.

Improving social skills can make people more confident in social situations and reduce anxiety. They may be better able to manage the negative thoughts and emotions that are part of social anxiety. Shavel Gordon is a young adult living with social anxiety and has experienced the challenge of improving her social skills. Over the years, Gordon has made steady progress and has learned to be patient with herself as she maneuvers social situations. "Throughout this process, I evaluated my progress after each social event, from which I noticed that many people also have awkward moments. So, I wasn't completely alone, and perhaps I wasn't always being judged as harshly as I thought," she recalls. Gordon offers encouragement to others who are practicing social skills: "Change is possible. No matter how difficult it seems. Improving your social skills may take some years, but taking your time is essential. You will eventually get there."[44]

## CHAPTER FOUR

# Living with Social Anxiety

Twenty-year-old Jolanta has lived with social anxiety for years. In school, she was unwilling to speak up in class and was harshly critical of her performance in every social situation. "I was always afraid of doing the wrong thing in a social situation, and I constantly preoccupied myself with questions like, 'Why am I like this? Why can't I just be like those who don't mind speaking up?' I'd immediately assume there's something wrong with me,"[45] she says. Stress and anxiety over potential social interactions hung over her daily.

Over the years, Jolanta has learned how important it is to take care of her mental health and be kind to herself. She tries not to compare herself to others and instead focuses on her interests and goals. As a result, Jolanta has become more confident and resilient. "Something that has definitely helped me build my self-esteem is discovering myself. My interests and values help build a solid foundation for my identity so that when an embarrassing situation arises (and believe me, it has been many, many times), I take it light-heartedly because I've grown confident in who I am,"[46] she explains.

For Jolanta, small steps have made a big difference. Making small changes in her life and slowly building her confidence have had a significant effect on her ability to manage her social anxiety. "It's crucial for you to understand that you don't have to take everything on at once. Instead, choose small steps that feel comfortable to you while still putting yourself out there,"[47] she suggests.

## Challenge Negative Thoughts

Many people find that one of the most important steps toward successfully living with social anxiety is being able to challenge and interrupt negative thoughts. People with social anxiety often dwell on what could possibly go wrong in social situations. They worry about saying something rude, tripping, spilling a drink on themselves, laughing at the wrong time, getting sick in front of others, or any number of things that could embarrass or humiliate them. Although these things do happen from time to time, people who can manage their anxiety have learned to keep them in perspective. They do not let negative thinking and worrying about "what ifs" overwhelm them.

When negative thoughts start creeping in, people can challenge and replace them with more positive thinking. They can start by asking themselves simple questions about the worrisome situation and giving honest answers. If they are going to meet new people for the first time, they might worry that they will say something to embarrass themselves or turn others away. They might see themselves making one mistake after another and regretting that they chose to engage with others. To prevent these negative thoughts from snowballing, people can ask themselves questions such as "What makes me think I will say something embarrassing?," "How many times have I been to a party and not done something embarrassing?," "What is the worst that could happen?," and "What would you tell a friend worrying about the same thing?" The answers can be calming and help those with social anxiety realize that the risk is not so great and the reward can be new, comfortable relationships.

## Small Changes and Realistic Goals

Trying to manage social anxiety can feel overwhelming. It is natural to avoid situations that cause stress and anxiety. However, consistently avoiding these situations can make social anxiety worse over time. The more people expose themselves to anxiety-inducing social situations, the more comfortable they will feel with social interactions in the future.

For Emily, a young adult with social anxiety, taking a test in a large classroom with many other students triggered severe anxiety. She worried that she would do or say something embarrassing and would be trapped in the room with everyone staring at her. She increasingly avoided these situations and started taking tests alone in a separate classroom. However, when she started college, Emily was determined to overcome her social anxiety. She practiced mindfulness exercises and breathing techniques to calm her fears until she felt ready to tackle the classroom. She knew she could do it when she successfully sat in a lecture with hundreds of students. "Since then, it got gradually easier to work through my social anxiety. I still have the intrusive thoughts . . . but once I showed myself that I *could* fight my fears, it got

*Mandatory group situations, such as taking a test with a large group of people, can trigger severe social anxiety. But these feelings can often be managed through small changes and realistic goals.*

easier to let go of them and even easier to ask for more help,"[48] she says.

It is perfectly acceptable to start with small changes and set realistic goals for oneself. For example, a small change could be making eye contact with a stranger or giving someone a compliment. With effort, small changes can add up to large changes and long-term goals.

After years of suffering with social anxiety, Julie hit rock bottom as a young adult in her thirties. Her anxiety had gotten so bad that she was afraid of almost everything. Going for a bike ride, taking a walk down the street, attending her son's baseball game, and any activity in which people could see her triggered anxiety and fear. At this point, Julie knew she needed to make changes in her life. She researched social anxiety disorder and started CBT. She relates how she slowly began exercises to challenge her negative thoughts and fears:

> "It got gradually easier to work through my social anxiety. I still have the intrusive thoughts . . . but once I showed myself that I could fight my fears, it got easier to let go of them and even easier to ask for more help."[48]
>
> —Emily, a young adult with social anxiety

I started out by doing small things. Driving and going places by myself (other than work) had been almost impossible. I started driving to the mall by myself. Step by little step, I was able to go into a department store and return an item without a receipt . . . even though I knew I would probably have to be assertive.

I would eat in the mall's food court by myself. I was afraid to do this, but I would tell myself rational things like "if people want to watch me eat, they have a problem" or "no one is looking at me, and it's OK."[49]

These affirmations helped Julie gain coping skills and change her negative mindset.

## Progressive Muscle Relaxation

One of anxiety's physical symptoms is tight muscles. Many people find that a practice called progressive muscle relaxation helps to ease muscle tightness and calms anxious thoughts. To start, a person sits in a comfortable position and focuses on breathing. The person tenses a muscle group, such as the right arm and hand, and holds it for several seconds. Then, the individual relaxes the muscles and lets go of any tension. Slowly, the person repeats this cycle for each muscle group throughout the body. For twenty-year-old Eve, progressive muscle relaxation is an easy way to calm anxious thoughts, especially when she feels overwhelmed. "Muscle tension is one way your body responds to feelings of anxiety. This technique is a way to own that tension and let it dissolve. It's something to focus on and distract yourself with," she explains. With regular practice, progressive muscle relaxation can help a person become more attuned to his or her body tension and learn how to release it.

Eve, "How I Use Progressive Muscle Relaxation for Anxiety," YoungMinds, October 26, 2020. www.youngminds.org.uk.

## Managing Daily Challenges

If people with anxiety know they will be attending a job interview or a work party, planning can help reduce some of the anxiety that might arise. They can think about the event and who will be attending. In advance, these individuals can come up with ideas on what to say or do. They may even try role-playing with a trusted friend or family member to practice conversations they might have. Planning and practicing before a social event are great ways to help a person feel more prepared.

For Rakshitha Arni Ravishankar, an adult with social anxiety, work-related parties are particularly stressful events. She relates how she manages her social anxiety at these events by planning before she goes:

> I personally dread them because I'm always unsure of how to initiate conversations beyond my work life—and be interesting at that. This lack of structure or predictability can feel

unnerving, especially with big social groups. The advice here is to make a simple structure for yourself ahead of these situations. Pick three to four people that you'd like to talk to. For instance, it could include your direct report, your boss, and the receptionist.

Choosing a few people to connect with can turn a large, intimidating gathering into a manageable experience. "A little structure can help you overthink less throughout the event,"[50] she explains.

Planning an exit strategy before an event or social gathering can also be helpful. People can decide what to do or where to go if they feel uncomfortable or overwhelmed. For example, they can plan to step outside or into the bathroom to grab a few minutes alone.

## Positive Self-Talk

Some people have found that positive self-talk is beneficial for managing social anxiety. Positive self-talk is an internal conversation people have with themselves that makes them feel good. People can use positive self-talk to remind themselves about their strengths, build confidence, think optimistically, and increase motivation. Some people repeat affirmations or mantras that encourage them before and during social situations. They might repeat phrases like "I can do this" or "I am comfortable in crowds" to themselves. Several studies have found that people who regularly use positive self-talk can better cope with mental and emotional stress.

Mehek Azra, a fifteen-year-old high school student in New York, uses positive self-talk to manage her social anxiety. "Talk to yourself the way you wish others would talk to you. Never disrespect yourself. Remind yourself that as much as you may think others are judging you, most of the time, they are just busy with themselves," she states. When walking through the mall and seeing a group of teenagers laugh, Mehek is tempted to think they are laughing at her. However, she turns to self-talk to give herself another explanation: "The teenagers in the mall laughed because one of their friends made a joke." When tempted to think a classmate is laughing at her, Mehek reassures herself with another explanation: "That one girl laughed when you were reading out loud because she and her friend were making inside jokes that did not involve you,"[51] she says.

> "Talk to yourself the way you wish others would talk to you. Never disrespect yourself. Remind yourself that as much as you may think others are judging you, most of the time, they are just busy with themselves."[51]
>
> —Mehek Azra, a teen with social anxiety

## Visualization

Some people practice visualization to manage their social anxiety. They visualize themselves walking into social situations with confidence. They visualize themselves interacting with others successfully and without causing themselves embarrassment. Through visualization, people can practice what it will feel like in social situations and feel like they are in control.

Social anxiety coach Katy Morin uses visualization to help herself and her clients manage their social anxiety. People can create

*Visualization can ease social anxiety. If you visualize yourself having a great time at an upcoming lunch with friends, you will have an easier time handling the situation in real life.*

## Coping by Counting

To calm anxious thoughts and feelings, some people use a diversion strategy that pairs counting with observations using the five senses. For example, they might count in their head five things that can be seen, four that can be felt, three that can be heard, two that can be smelled, and one that can be tasted. This exercise engages the mind in the moment and distracts it from worrying. It gives a person something to do instead of worrying and being preoccupied with anxious thoughts. Sometimes counting works quickly to relieve anxiety. Other times, it may take longer and need to be repeated one or more times. Counting also can be done quickly and discreetly, whenever a person needs to calm down in a social or public setting. It is a simple tool that can be used in crowded spaces like restaurants, trains, or airplanes, where other anxiety-relieving exercises might be more difficult to do.

visualization in many ways, such as writing it down, saying it out loud, or imagining a television scene. According to Morin,

> It makes no difference to your brain if you are in the situation or picturing it in your head—the emotions you feel will be the same. This means that when you are practicing these visualizations, you can genuinely see yourself being successful in social situations. You can imagine yourself interacting with people in a way that is comfortable and enjoyable—and all this while sitting alone at home.[52]

She notes that the more that one practices visualization, the easier it becomes.

## Build a Support Network

Having a solid support system is an essential part of living successfully with social anxiety. Some people find support from family members and friends. Others join support groups with people facing similar challenges. No matter where support comes from, talking with a trusted individual can help a person cope with and manage the daily challenges of social anxiety.

Twenty-two-year-old Emily did not have a support system when she was dealing with crippling social anxiety at school. Looking back on her experiences, Emily wishes she had confided in a trusted friend or family member:

> Going through all of this, I felt so alone. I was too embarrassed by the side effects of my social anxiety to tell anyone what I was going through. If I did say anything, I'd sugarcoat it and only tell a version of the truth that I could handle admitting. For me, that's where I first went wrong. I really wish I could tell 17-year-old Emily to just tell someone. Believe me, it feels so much better to get your worries out of your head and be honest about what you're going through. You're likely to find that other people have similar "weird" or "embarrassing" worries too.[53]

Gigi, a twenty-five-year-old with social anxiety, knows firsthand how helpful a solid support system can be. She relies on a trusted circle of friends when her anxiety surfaces. "I opened up to a few of my friends. . . and told them that last time I felt anxious and that I hope it won't be as bad next time," she says. Gigi plans to be even more open in the future when she is struggling. "Next time, I will be honest with the friends around me and ask for help if I am feeling anxious—I don't need to hide how I'm feeling. I have also asked one of them to come for a walk with me away from the [larger] group [of people] if I say I need it,"[54] she says.

## One Day at a Time

Garret Winton, a twenty-two-year-old nursing assistant from Tallahassee, Florida, manages his social anxiety one day at a time. Winton first noticed his social anxiety in middle school. In college, Winton was doing well managing his anxiety, but then the COVID-19 pandemic struck in 2020. As people tried to stop the virus from spreading by limiting social contact, the resulting lockdowns and social isolation caused Winton's anxiety to flare again. He began to experience recurring panic attacks that caused him to hyperventilate.

Despite this setback, Winton was determined to regain control of his social anxiety. He has steadily worked to manage his fears and anxious thoughts. To accomplish this, Winton spends time on activities that he knows help calm his anxiety, such as exercise. He has also been making a purposeful effort to answer texts from his friends and not ignore them. Recently, a friend texted Winton and asked if he wanted to meet for dinner. As Winton drove to the restaurant, his heartbeat accelerated. Anxious thoughts began to pop up in his mind. From the parking lot, he could see his friends inside the restaurant, but Winton stayed in the car and waited for a few minutes. He reassured himself and repeated a phrase he had found to be calming, "You can do this."[55] A few moments later, Winton felt calm enough to leave the car and walk to the restaurant entrance. He went inside and pulled a chair to a table with his friends. It was a small step, but it was progress for that day.

Take it one day at a time when managing social anxiety. Overcome one small challenge every day, like answering texts promptly, exercising, or meeting up with a friend.

# Living Well with Social Anxiety

Social anxiety is a serious mental health condition that can disrupt every part of a person's life. Yet social anxiety can be managed. Strategies and treatment to overcome social anxiety may look different for every individual and can include therapy, medication, lifestyle changes, and mindfulness practices. With time and patience, many people learn to manage and overcome social anxiety. "If we step back and look beyond the fact that those with social anxiety care about what other people think of them, we realize that they simply care about people. There is a great deal of empathy and need for connection there. We can tap into that. The goal is to slowly—and at your own pace—experiment with new ways of navigating social situations,"[56] advises clinical psychologist Ellen Hendriksen.

> "Acknowledging my mental health struggles has helped me see them for what they are: mental health struggles that don't define who I want to show up as."[57]
>
> —Rakshitha Arni Ravishankar, an adult with social anxiety

It has taken Ravishankar a lot of time and effort to learn how to manage her social anxiety. She comments,

> From personal experience, I know that none of these strategies are easy. It takes time, patience, and deliberate effort to unlearn your instinctive thoughts and behaviors and reassure yourself. That said, I also know that working through these feelings will be worth it. Doing so has helped me build self-compassion and move away from seeing myself solely as a "good" or a "bad" person. Most importantly, acknowledging my mental health struggles has helped me see them for what they are: mental health struggles that don't define who I want to show up as.[57]

# SOURCE NOTES

## Introduction: A Struggle to Be Social

1. Jamie Factor, "Writing Saved Me," Anxiety & Depression Association of America, June 24, 2023. https://adaa.org.
2. Factor, "Writing Saved Me."
3. Factor, "Writing Saved Me."
4. Factor, "Writing Saved Me."
5. Thomas A. Richards, "What Is It Like to Live with Social Anxiety?," Social Anxiety Institute. https://socialanxietyinstitute.org.
6. Quoted in Maria Kohut, "4 Top Tips for Coping with Social Anxiety," Medical News Today, August 30, 2019. www.medicalnewstoday.com.
7. Quoted in Cleveland Clinic, "Need Help Overcoming Social Anxiety? 6 Tips from an Expert," November 21, 2021. https://health.clevelandclinic.org.

## Chapter One: Understanding Social Anxiety

8. Quoted in Eduardo Medina, "How Young People's Social Anxiety Has Worsened in the Pandemic," *New York Times,* September 27, 2021. www.nytimes.com.
9. Quoted in Emily Laurence, "How to Overcome Social Anxiety, According to Experts," *Forbes*, July 26, 2023. www.forbes.com.
10. Quoted in Laurence, "How to Overcome Social Anxiety, According to Experts."
11. Quoted in Columbian College of Arts and Sciences, "Fear of Failing: The Secrets Behind Social Anxiety," March 8, 2023. https://columbian.gwu.edu.
12. Ellen Hendriksen, "Unpacking Social Anxiety," Psychwire. https://psychwire.com.
13. Sophie, "My Experience of Social Anxiety at University," YoungMinds, August 17, 2020. www.youngminds.org.uk.
14. Quoted in Medina, "How Young People's Social Anxiety Has Worsened in the Pandemic."
15. Quoted in Cleveland Clinic, "Need Help Overcoming Social Anxiety?"
16. Paddy, "How I Learnt to Cope with Sports Performance Anxiety," YoungMinds, October 24, 2022. www.youngminds.org.uk.

17. Quoted in Zameena Mejia, "What Is Social Anxiety Disorder?," *Forbes*, July 31, 2023. www.forbes.com.
18. Quoted in Columbian College of Arts and Sciences, "Fear of Failing."
19. Victoria Williams, "What Happened When My 'Friends' Turned Against Me Because of My Anxiety," *Anxiety* (blog), The Mighty, February 1, 2019. https://themighty.com.
20. Quoted in Beyond Blue, "Social Anxiety: I'm Terrified of Dating," *Not Alone* (podcast), September 12, 2022. www.beyondblue.org.au.

## Chapter Two: Treatments and Strategies for Social Anxiety

21. Quoted in Cleveland Clinic, "Need Help Overcoming Social Anxiety?"
22. Quoted in Laurence, "How to Overcome Social Anxiety, According to Experts."
23. Kristen Rogers, "After Years of Debilitating Social Anxiety, a Special Tool Changed My Life," CNN, April 1, 2022. www.cnn.com.
24. Karmen Smith, "Exposure Therapy for Social Anxiety," Talkspace, September 22, 2023. www.talkspace.com.
25. Quoted in Meagan Drillinger, "How to Make Friends When You Have Social Anxiety," Healthline, February 25, 2020. www.healthline.com.
26. Quoted in Drillinger, "How to Make Friends When You Have Social Anxiety."
27. Quoted in Sean Grover, "Social Anxiety? 3 Reasons to Try Group Therapy," *Anxiety* (blog), *Psychology Today*, January 11, 2019. www.psychologytoday.com.
28. Quoted in Laurence, "How to Overcome Social Anxiety, According to Experts."
29. Quoted in Laurence, "How to Overcome Social Anxiety, According to Experts."
30. Ian Chew, "Social Anxiety in College: 5 Things I Wish I Had Known," Grown and Flown, January 22, 2023. https://grownandflown.com.
31. Quoted in Beyond Blue, "Finding Answers to Anxiety: Amy's Story." www.beyondblue.org.au.
32. Quoted in Beyond Blue, "Finding Answers to Anxiety."
33. Claire Eastham, "A Day in the Life of Someone with Social Anxiety," Healthline, April 18, 2019. www.healthline.com.

## Chapter Three: Improving Social Skills

34. Arlin Cuncic, "How to Socialize When You Have Social Anxiety Disorder," Verywell Mind, September 26, 2023. www.verywellmind.com.
35. Arlin Cuncic, "An Overview of Social Skills Training," Verywell Mind, January 16, 2024. www.verywellmind.com.

36. Claire Eastham, "SOS! I Have Social Anxiety and Know Absolutely No One at This Party," Healthline, April 18, 2019. www.healthline.com.
37. Arlin Cuncic, "Small Talk Topics," Verywell Mind, February 15, 2023. www.verywellmind.com.
38. Arlin Cuncic, "What Is Active Listening?," Verywell Mind, November 9, 2022. www.verywellmind.com.
39. Office of the Ombuds, "Active Listening," Boston University. www.bumc.bu.edu.
40. Rachel Wells, "Active Listening Skills: What They Are and Why They're Important," *Forbes*, September 4, 2023. www.forbes.com.
41. Kendra Cherry, "10 Tips for Improving Your Nonverbal Communication," Verywell Mind, December 12, 2022. www.verywellmind.com.
42. Julie, "My Social Anxiety and How I Overcame It," Social Anxiety Institute. https://socialanxietyinstitute.org.
43. Quoted in Anxiety & Depression Association of America, "Social Skills Training (SST): A Tool for Social Anxiety Disorder: In Conversation with 2023 ADAA Annual Conference Presenters," *Triumphing Through Science, Treatment, and Education* (blog), May 22, 2023. https://adaa.org.
44. Shavel Gordon, "My Uphill Battle with Social Anxiety Disorder," Active Care Group, May 11, 2023. https://activecaregroup.co.uk.

# Chapter Four: Living with Social Anxiety

45. Jolanta, "How to Manage Social Anxiety at School," YoungMinds, January 16, 2023. www.youngminds.org.uk.
46. Jolanta, "How to Manage Social Anxiety at School."
47. Jolanta, "How to Manage Social Anxiety at School."
48. Quoted in YoungMinds, "Coping with Social Phobia," March 19, 2021. www.youngminds.org.uk.
49. Julie, "My Social Anxiety and How I Overcame It."
50. Rakshitha Arni Ravishankar, "How I Manage My Social Anxiety at Work," *Harvard Business Review,* April 12, 2022. https://hbr.org.
51. Mehek Azra, "What It's Like to Be a Teen with Social Anxiety," Skipping Stones, March 23, 2021. www.skippingstones.org.
52. Katy Morin, "An Antidote to Social Anxiety," *Better Humans,* November 12, 2023. https://betterhumans.pub.
53. Quoted in YoungMinds, "Coping with Social Phobia."
54. Quoted in YoungMinds, "Coping with Social Anxiety as Lockdown Eases," July 24, 2020. www.youngminds.org.uk.
55. Quoted in Medina, "How Young People's Social Anxiety Has Worsened in the Pandemic."
56. Quoted in Ravishankar, "How I Manage My Social Anxiety at Work."
57. Ravishankar, "How I Manage My Social Anxiety at Work."

# GETTING HELP AND INFORMATION

## Books

A.W. Buckey, *Dealing with Anxiety Disorder*. San Diego: ReferencePoint, 2020.

Ellen Hendriksen, *How to Be Yourself: Quiet Your Inner Critic and Rise Above Social Anxiety*. New York: St. Martin's Griffin, 2019.

Thomas McDonagh and Jon Patrick Hatcher, *The Teen Anxiety Guidebook: Improve Self-Esteem, Discover New Coping Skills, and Relieve Social Anxiety, Worry, and Panic Attacks*. Berkeley, CA: Bloom, 2023.

Barbara Sheen, *Teen Guide to Managing Stress and Anxiety*. San Diego: ReferencePoint, 2022.

Jacqueline Sperling, *Find Your Fierce: How to Put Social Anxiety in Its Place*. Washington, DC: Magination, 2021.

Bridget Flynn Walker, *Social Anxiety Relief for Teens: A Step-by-Step CBT Guide to Feel Confident & Comfortable in Any Situation*. Oakland, CA: New Harbinger, 2021.

## Internet Sources

Andrea Brognano, "Social Anxiety in Teens: Symptoms, Causes & Treatment," Choosing Therapy, January 13, 2023. www.choosingtherapy.com.

Eduardo Medina, "How Young People's Social Anxiety Has Worsened in the Pandemic," *New York Times*, September 27, 2021. www.nytimes.com.

Nemours Teens Health, "Social Anxiety," May 2023. www.kidshealth.org.

Lindsey Tanner, "Mindfulness Worked as Well for Anxiety as Drug in Study," Associated Press, November 9, 2022. www.apnews.com.

## Websites

**American Psychiatric Association**
www.psychiatry.org
The American Psychiatric Association is an organization of physicians working together to ensure humane care and effective treatment for all persons with mental disorders. Its website includes a special section on mental health resources for families and information about anxiety disorders, including social anxiety disorder.

**American Psychological Association**
www.apa.org
The American Psychological Association represents American psychologists, who study and treat human behavior. The association's website features information and resources for psychologists, health care workers, and the public about various mental health topics, including social anxiety disorder.

**Anxiety & Depression Association of America (ADAA)**
https://adaa.org
The ADAA is a nonprofit organization dedicated to the prevention, treatment, and cure of anxiety, depression, and other co-occurring disorders. Its website features news, information, videos, and personal stories about anxiety.

**Centers for Disease Control and Prevention (CDC)**
www.cdc.gov
The CDC is the premier public health agency in the United States. Its website includes the latest information about mental health disorders, treatment, and research, including anxiety disorders. It has links to other government centers, such as the National Institute of Mental Health, where more information can be found.

**Mental Health America**
https://mhanational.org
Mental Health America is an advocacy group for people with mental illnesses and their families. Its website features many resources, including an interactive tool to assist in finding mental health help, information on support groups, and mental health screening tools.

### National Alliance on Mental Illness (NAMI)
www.nami.org
NAMI is an advocacy group for people with mental illnesses and has local chapters across the country. Its website offers a variety of resources, including information about mental health conditions such as anxiety disorders, support groups, helplines, and more.

### National Institute of Mental Health (NIMH)
www.nimh.nih.gov
The NIMH is the federal government's chief funding agency for mental health research in America. The institute's website provides a variety of information and fact sheets on mental health disorders, including anxiety disorders, treatments, and the latest mental health research.

# INDEX

*Note: Boldface page numbers indicate illustrations.*

acceptance and commitment therapy (ACT), 27
active listening skills, **36**–38
American Psychiatric Association, 58
American Psychological Association, 58
Anxiety & Depression Association of America (ADAA), 6, 58
assertive communication, 39–**41**
Azra, Mehek, 48–**49**

benzodiazepines, 25
beta-blockers, 25
body language
  negative, 38–39
  positive, 39
brain-derived neurotrophic factor (BDNF), 15

Centers for Disease Control and Prevention (CDC), 58
Chapman, Kevin, 9, 21, 26–27, 28
Cherry, Kendra, 39
Chew, Ian, 28
cognitive behavioral therapy (CBT), 20–22
communication skills, 33
  active listening and, **36**–38
  assertiveness and, 39–**41**
  empathy and, 38
  nonverbal, 38–39
Cornell Weill School of Medicine, 15
cortisol, 28–**29**
counting, as diversion strategy, 50
Cuncic, Arlin, 33–**34**, 35, 37

Eastham, Claire, 31, 35
empathy, **36**
exercise, 28
exposure therapy, 22–**23**
eye contact, 37, 38

Factor, Jamie, 4–5

Goodman, Fallon, 9–10, 17
Gordon, Shavel, 42
group therapy, 25–26
gut microbes, 14

Halstead, Mailae, 9
Hayes, Steven, 27
Hendriksen, Ellen, 10, 53
Hidalgo-Gonzales, Nanichi, 12

introversion, 17, 32
  social anxiety *vs.*, 18
  use of social skills and, 32

Lev, Avigail, 27
lifestyle changes, 28–**29**

managing social anxiety, 43–44, 53
  building support network, 50–51
  dealing with negative thoughts, 44
  managing daily challenges, 47–48
  positive self-talk, 48–**49**
  progressive muscle relaxation, 47
  setting realistic goals, 44–46
  visualization, **49**–50
medication, **24**–25
meditation, 27–28
Mental Health America, 59
mindfulness/mindful meditation, 27–28
Morin, Katy, **49**–50
muscle relaxation, progressive, 47

National Alliance on Mental Illness (NAMI), 59
National Institute of Mental Health (NIMH), 59
Neal-Barnett, Angela, 15
nonverbal communication skills, 38–39

Page, Nevandria, 8
performance-based social anxiety, **13**–14
positive self-talk, 48
Potter, Dawn, 7, 13, 20–21
progressive muscle relaxation, 47

Ravishankar, Rakshitha Arni, 18, 47–48, 53

Richards, Thomas A., 5–6
risk factors, 15–17
Rogers, Kristen, 21–22

selective serotonin reuptake inhibitors (SSRIs), 24, 25
self-talk, positive, 48
serotonin, **24**
serotonin-norepinephrine reuptake inhibitors (SNRIs), 25
Shaw, Victoria, 22–**23**
smiling, 40
Smith, Karmen, 22
social anxiety/social anxiety disorder
  art of conversation and, 33–**34**
  causes of, 15
  everyday social interactions and, 5–**6**
  introversion *vs.*, 18
  performance-based, **13**–14
  prevalence of, **6**
  risk factors for, 15–17
  signs/symptoms of, 10–13
  *See also* managing social anxiety; treatment
social skills, 32–33
  active listening, **36**–38
  communication, 33–35
  nonverbal communication, 38–39
  smiling, 40
social skills training (SST), **41**–42
support groups, 26–27
support networks, 50–51

treatment, 7
   acceptance and commitment therapy, 27
   cognitive behavioral therapy, 20–22
   exposure therapy, 22–**23**
   group therapy, 25–26
   lifestyle changes, 28–**29**
   medication, **24**–25
   mindfulness meditation, 27–28
   psychotherapy, 20
   role of health care professionals, 30
   support groups, 26–27

visualization, 49–50

websites, 58–59
Wells, Rachel, 37–38
Williams, Victoria, 17–18
Winton, Garret, 51–**52**

Yale University, 15

# PICTURE CREDITS

Cover: RyFlip/Shutterstock.com

6: Mandy Godbehear/Shutterstock.com
11: Inna Reznik/Shutterstock.com
13: Halfpoint/Shutterstock.com
16: MalikNalik/Shutterstock.com
23: Tero Vesalainen/Shutterstock.com
24: Rocketclips, Inc./Shutterstock.com
29: Jacek Chabraszewski/Shutterstock.com
34: silverkblackstock/Shutterstock.com
36: Motortion Films/Shutterstock.com
41: VH-studio/Shutterstock.com
45: Ground Picture/Shutterstock.com
49: Lucky Business/Shutterstock.com
52: Monkey Business Images/Shutterstock.com

# ABOUT THE AUTHOR

Carla Mooney is the author of many books for young adults and children. She lives in Pittsburgh, Pennsylvania, with her husband and three children.